every teenager's
little black book
of hard to find information

by blaine bartel

every teenager's
little black book
of hard to find information

by blaine bartel

Harrison House
Tulsa, Oklahoma

06 05 04 03   10 9 8 7 6 5 4

Every Teenager's Little Black Book of Hard-To-Find Information
ISBN 1-57794-457-7
Copyright © 2002 by Blaine Bartel
P.O. Box 691923
Tulsa, Oklahoma 74179

Published by Harrison House, Inc.
P.O. Box 35035
Tulsa, Oklahoma 74153

contents

Relationships

School

contents (continued)

Self-Esteem

Money

contents (continued)

Authority

Success

[RELATIONSHIPS**]**

6 REASONS TO SAY NO TO PREMARITAL SEX

The Bible teaches us in 1 Corinthians 6:18 to flee sexual immorality. God is not a "Grinch" trying to steal all the fun out of your teenage years. He wants to protect you and prepare you for a wonderful marriage relationship where sexuality will have its perfect place.

Here are 6 reasons to say no until then.

1. You will close the door on sin and its destructive nature.

2. The thought of raising a baby while you're a teenager will never enter your mind.

3. You will never have a doctor tell you that you've contracted a sexually transmitted disease.

4. Friends and classmates will never see compromise in your life that will cause them to talk behind your back and lose respect for who you are.

5. God will be able to trust you with His very best as you give Him your very best.

6. You will never have to deal with "ghosts of relationships past" in your marriage relationship.

6 REASONS TO BREAK UP WITH SOMEONE

I discourage you from "going out" or "dating" too early. The Bible has much to say about developing good friendships but nothing about dating. As you grow older and a good friendship develops into a romantic relationship, be careful to keep things on the right track.

In case you're not sure, here are 6 reasons to break off a relationship that has gotten off track.

1. If you are being pressured in any way to take the relationship to a "physical" level, know it is inappropriate.

2. If you are verbally, mentally, or physically abused in any way, get out of the relationship—quickly.

3. If your partner doesn't show the spiritual drive and Christian attributes that you know are necessary to be strong for Christ, it's time to let go.

4. If you feel used in any way for what you have, give, own, or provide, don't stay in the relationship. Be sure the person likes (or loves) you. Period.

5. If you find the person to be a liar, don't stick around. Trust can only be built on truth.

6. If the person breaks up with you, let go. Seriously. There are many fish in the sea, and you may have just gotten rid of "Jaws," so move on!

5 FRIENDS THAT WILL TAKE YOU DOWN

The Bible tells us that those who walk with the wise will be wise, but the companion of fools will be destroyed. (Prov. 13:20.) Here are 5 different kinds of "friends" that can destroy your relationship with the Lord.

1. **The mocker:** the friend who always makes fun of spiritual things.

2. **The doubter:** the friend who believes and talks about the worst; usually the last to acknowledge what God can do.

3. **The compromiser:** the friend who goes to church and talks a good talk but, more often than not, does not back it up with a life that honors God.

4. **The proud:** the friend who thinks he or she is more spiritual than you or anyone else and constantly displays a critical attitude about everyone else's "lack of commitment."

5. **The gossip:** the friend who always "talks down" other people around you. If a person says negative things to

you about his or her other friends, what is the person saying to them about you?

7 WAYS TO AVOID PREMARITAL SEX

It's one thing to know that we should flee sexual immorality, but you may be wondering, "How do I do it?" Here are 7 ways that you can avoid the sin that can destroy you and your future.

1. Sexual sin starts in the mind, so win the war there first by studying the Bible. Fill your mind with God's Word.

2. Stay in church. The more you hear the Word and stay close to other Christians, the better you will keep your focus on spiritual things.

3. Don't ever go out alone with a person you know will tempt you or easily give in to sexual sin.

4. Don't allow yourself to be alone with the opposite sex in a place where temptation is easily fostered.

5. Stay away from sexually suggestive books, magazines, photos, or Web sites that will stir up sexual desires.

6. Build relationships of accountability with parents and strong Christian friends. When going through a trying time, let them know and ask for their help.

7. Make up your mind. Never retreat. Let every new friend
    you meet know you are committed to sexual purity.

5 QUESTIONS REAL FRIENDS
SHOULD ASK EACH OTHER

A smart person is known by the good questions he or she asks. When Jesus was 12 years old, He was found in the temple asking questions of the teachers of the law.

Here are 5 questions that good friends should ask each other.

1. How can I be a better friend to you?

2. Are there any traits, attitudes, or actions you see in my life that hinder my success?

3. What gifts and characteristics do you recognize as strengths in my life?

4. How can I pray for you at this time in your life?

5. What has God shown you in His Word lately?

[SCHOOL]

4 THINGS TO LEARN AT SCHOOL
THAT NO ONE TEACHES

Make no mistake. Your teachers will give you important information that will prove valuable in the days to come: math, history, science, and trigonometry—okay, at least most of it will be valuable.

There are also some great things you can learn at school that your teachers will not actually show you. Here they are:

1. **Learn the art of discipline.** Take advantage of your free time during or between classes to finish your assignments.

2. **Learn to negotiate.** Develop your skills working with teachers, coaches, and fellow students to "give and take" in order to reach your goals.

3. **Learn to say no.** Classmates will ask you to cheat, lie, gossip, lust, vandalize—you name it. Put no in your vocabulary.

4. **Learn to love without respect of persons.** You will meet people every day who don't appeal to you. Love them with Christ's love in spite of your feelings.

7 KEYS TO REMEMBERING
WHAT YOU STUDIED

When you think of school you may think of "tests." The key to passing is the ability to remember what you learned a long time ago, even if you were only half awake and it was a Monday morning.

So here are some keys to doing just that.

1. Actually listen to the teacher while in the class.

2. Take good notes—even if your mind tells you it has the ability to "remember all things."

3. Talk with a friend or parent later that day about what you learned—even if it's spiced with a tinge of humor.

4. Remind yourself about all the rewards that come with a good grade.

5. When studying, write your key points down again.

6. When studying, say your key points aloud multiple times.

7. Pray and ask God to bring those things you've learned back to your remembrance. (John 14:26.)

5 THINGS YOU'LL WISH YOU'D LEARNED
10 YEARS AFTER GRADUATING

It's been more than 10 years since I got out of high school and jumped into the "real world." Here's what I found out. No matter how bad you thought school was at the time, you will usually only remember the good times. Here are some things you should do before you graduate.

1. **Keep a "highlights" journal.** You don't have to write in it every day—just when cool things happen.

2. **Take lots of pictures or video.** It isn't just for you, but for your kids. The one thing my kids love to ask about is what I was like in high school.

3. **Share your faith in Jesus with your friends.** You may think you'll be friends forever, but you won't. Some move away, others become too busy, some die, and others just drop right out. Seize the day! (2 Cor. 6:2.)

4. **Experiment.** Try out different sports, new hobbies and interests, different classes, fresh challenges. You

may catch on to something great you didn't know existed!

5. **Study hard, and work hard.** The discipline you develop today will bring you the rewards you'll want a decade from now. (2 Tim. 2:15.)

4 WAYS TO MAKE SCHOOL GO BY QUICKLY

Why is it that when you're having fun, time seems to fly by, but when you get to school it seems the clock has stopped or is moving backwards? Simple: when you enjoy something, you don't care how long it takes.

Here are 4 ways to make school more enjoyable.

1. **Set goals for your grades and achievement.** If you have a vision and you focus on getting there, you'll move at a different pace. (Phil. 3:14.)

2. **Create personal competitions in your classes and with your homework.** As you work on each project, motivate yourself with a challenge of some kind. Set yourself up against the clock, your previous grade, or even a fellow student.

3. **Get involved in something at school you can really can look forward to.** It may be sports, a club activity, cheerleading, school council—in short, do something you like.

4. **Go to school each day with a good mental attitude.** Your mind and your decisions control your

emotions. Proverbs 23:7 NKJV says, "As he thinks in his heart, so is he." Decide every day, "This is the day the Lord has made—I will rejoice and be glad in it!" (Ps. 118:24.)

6 STUDENTS CLASSMATES LOVE TO HATE

A big part of enjoying school includes having friends you look forward to seeing every day. The Bible says that a person who wants friends must show oneself friendly. (Prov. 18:24.) Don't allow your attitudes and actions to cause you to be someone the other students hate to be around.

1. **The pity seeker** feels sorry for him- or herself, trying to get the attention and pity of others.

2. **The bragger** talks about him- or herself, what *"I have,"* what *"I can do,"* and what *"I know."*

3. **The loner** isolates him- or herself from others, making it impossible for others to get to know them.

4. **The gossip** always talks bad about others in the school, including those who are supposedly his or her friends.

5. **The roller-coaster** goes up and down emotionally. One minute they are happy and a minute later they are crying.

6. **The bully** constantly demeans and picks one person that they perceive to be weaker than him- or herself.

[SELF ESTEEM]

5 ROADS TO POPULARITY WITHOUT LOSING YOUR REPUTATION

Everyone wants to be popular. Popularity isn't a bad thing. In fact, Jesus was very popular during much of His ministry. He never compromised His character or morals to gain acceptance. You can become popular by making both bad choices and good ones.

Here are 5 roads to popularity while maintaining your integrity.

1. **Be a kind person.** You will never be short on friends.

2. **When you do something, do it with all your might.** Excellence draws a crowd.

3. **Promote others and their accomplishments, not your own.** God will then be able to exalt you.

4. **Dare to dream big and pray for the seemingly impossible.** People are drawn to those filled with hope and faith.

5. **Stand up for what is right.** Our world today is desperately searching for real heroes.

7 WORDS TO REMOVE FROM
YOUR VOCABULARY

The Bible speaks about the power of words in relationship to your personal self-esteem. It says, "A wholesome tongue is a tree of life" (Prov. 15:4). Your words will bring life if they are good, but destruction if they are not. Here are 7 words you should eliminate from your vocabulary right now.

1. **Can't.** You can do all things through Christ who strengthens you. (Phil 4:13.)

2. **Never.** All things are possible to those who believe. (Mark 9:23.)

3. **Quit.** "Let us not grow weary while doing good, for in due season we shall reap if we do not lose heart" (Gal. 6:9 NKJV).

4. **Depressed.** "Rejoice in the Lord always: and again I say, Rejoice" (Phil. 4:4).

5. **Hate.** The Holy Ghost sheds the love of God abroad in our hearts. (Rom. 5:5.)

6. **Doubt.** "So then faith comes by hearing, and hearing by the Word of God" (Rom 10:17 NKJV).

7. **Broke.** My God shall supply all of your needs by His riches in glory in Christ Jesus. (Phil. 4:19.)

4 FEARS YOU MUST CONQUER EVERY DAY

Fear is the primary tactic of your enemy, the devil. All through the Bible, we are told to "fear not." Fear will immobilize you and stop you from reaching your goals and full potential. You conquer your fears by studying, speaking, and acting on the Bible, God's Word. When you do, you will conquer these 4 kinds of fear every day.

1. **Fear of failure.** This lie tells you God is not strong enough to help you succeed, and it is perhaps the greatest attack of fear.

2. **Fear of the future.** This lie compels you to believe God is unable to see what lies ahead for you and to direct you in every step. (Ps. 37:23.)

3. **Fear of the past.** This haunting deception says that because of where you or your family has come from, God is unable to make everything good today. (2 Cor. 5:17.)

4. **Fear of comparison.** This lie tries to talk you into believing God favors someone else more because that

person appears to be doing better than you are. The enemy wants you to believe God has given up on you.

6 THINGS YOU MUST BELIEVE
ABOUT YOURSELF

You will eventually become a product of what you believe. All great athletes, presidents, pastors, and corporate CEOs arrived where they are because they believed they could before anyone else believed in them.

Here are 6 things you must believe about yourself.

1. I have been given power over the devil. (1 John 4:4.)

2. I have been given power over every circumstance in my life. (Mark 11:23.)

3. I have a strong body that has been healed by the stripes taken on Jesus' back. (Matt. 8:17.)

4. I have the ability to control my mind and cast out evil thoughts. (2 Cor. 10:4,5.)

5. I am poised for success and will not accept any defeat as final. (1 Cor. 15:57.)

6. I hate sin but love all people and have favor everywhere I go. (Prov. 12:2.)

5 HABITS OF HAPPY TEENAGERS

God wants you to be happy and enjoy life. That doesn't mean you will never experience trials or tough times. Here are 5 habits you can develop as a young person that will cause you to keep your joy through even the darkest hours.

1. **Regularly reading and meditating (thinking and pondering) on God's Word**. (Ps. 119:105.) This will energize your joy!

2. **Steadily communing with God.** "Communion" comes from the word "communicate." That's it! Talk to God, praise Him, and give Him your requests and cares.

3. **Vision thinking.** Find out what God has gifted you in. Take time to seek Him for your career and ambitions. Take one step at a time as you grow to get there.

4. **Singing a good song aloud!** God made us to sing. Not all of us sound that good, but it doesn't matter. Find songs and worship music that inspire you for good, and sing! (Ps. 95:1.)

5. **Attending church weekly.** Stay connected to good friends, strong mentors, and caring pastors who will help you stay on track.

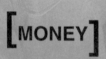

[MONEY]

6 CAREERS YOU CAN START IN YOUR TEENS

While your youth is a time to have fun and enjoy life, it is also a time to learn the value of work and ambition. The Bible has much to say about the importance of working diligently.

Here are 6 careers that you can embark on right now.

1. **Newspaper business.** Throw a paper route, and discover the satisfaction of getting a job done early.

2. **Investment broker.** There are companies that will take investment capital of just $50. Learn how the market works, and start investing a little at a time.

3. **Graphic arts.** If you have a bent for drawing and art, offer your assistance to those in need now. I know 14- and 15-year-olds who design logos and Web sites for companies and churches.

4. **Film and video production.** With an inexpensive camera and some software you can be in the "movie" biz. My son began to be paid for his projects when he was just 15 years old.

5. **Lawn care.** If you have a mower and a weed-eater, distribute flyers in your neighborhood and sign accounts to cut and trim grass after school and all summer.

6. **Child care.** Make yourself available to families for quality baby-sitting services. Be a good one, because they are hard to come by!

4 REASONS YOU'LL HAVE MORE
BY GIVING AWAY

Of course, we know that the Bible tells us to give a tithe (one-tenth) of our income to our local church, and offerings after the tithe to worthy causes. (Mal. 3:10,11.) There are at least 4 reasons you'll have more after you give.

1. The Bible teaches that giving is like planting a seed. Every seed produces a huge multiplication of its kind. (2 Cor 9:10.)

2. God promises to open heaven's windows and pour out blessings that you cannot possibly contain. (Mal. 3:10.)

3. Other people are naturally (and supernaturally) compelled to bless those who are unselfish in their giving. (Luke 6:38.)

4. Giving puts your faith in action, and faith is always rewarded abundantly by God. (Heb. 11:6.)

5 INVESTMENTS EVERY TEENAGER
SHOULD MAKE

An investment is something you contribute to without always seeing a quick or immediate return, trusting that its long-term results will be great.

Here are 5 investments you can't afford not to make.

1. **Invest in your church.** The church is the vehicle by which the Gospel can go forth. Commit to tithe right now.

2. **Invest in missions.** Find a person or ministry successfully reaching the lost, and help out by giving or going.

3. **Invest in your financial future.** Open a savings or money market account, and put something in it every month.

4. **Invest in your career.** Find your greatest interest in life (that can make you money), and read books on how to succeed in that area.

5. **Invest in your vocabulary.** Words are powerful. Learn new ones all the time, using them to be a better communicator, negotiator, and salesperson.

6 THINGS YOU'D BETTER KNOW
ABOUT MONEY

The Bible has literally hundreds of passages that discuss the issue of money. Next to God, it may well be the most powerful force in the earth. You had better know these 6 things about money.

1. It is not the root of all evil. Many say it is, but actually the Bible says, "The love of money is the root of all evil" (1 Tim. 6:10). That is a big difference.

2. No, it can't buy you love. It cannot purchase the love every human soul yearns for—the unconditional love of Jesus Christ.

3. You can have money and still be spiritual. The Bible commands Christians who are rich to be generous— not to take a vow of poverty. (1 Tim. 6:17-19.)

4. Money will come to those who work hard and plan carefully. (Prov. 21:5.)

5. Your good name and reputation for integrity are more important than a quick dollar. (Prov. 22:1.)

6. Don't seek money. Seek God and His wisdom. (Matt 6:33.) Solomon asked God for His wisdom, and everything else came to him!

3 THINGS MONEY WILL DO AND
3 THINGS MONEY WON'T DO

Money can make many things happen for you, but there are a few things that it cannot do for you. Learning to distinguish the difference may be one of the most important lessons you could ever learn.

Here are 3 things money can do for you.

1. **It can multiply.** When you learn how to give and receive, buy and sell, invest and grow—money will multiply. (Luke 6:38.)

2. **It can be an instrument of love.** When you use it to help the poor, the needy, or the lost, it becomes God's love in motion.

3. **It can be a testimony.** As God has blessed and provided for you, give Him the glory and others will see God's goodness.

Here are 3 things money can't do for you.

1. **It can't soothe your conscience.** Giving it away will never bring forgiveness of sin or relief of guilt. Only Christ can do that.

2. **It can't replace your work for God.** Every Christian is called to actively serve in God's kingdom in some way. Just giving in the offering isn't enough.

3. **It can't go to heaven with you.** Don't hoard it. Make the best possible use of it while you're here!

[AUTHORITY]

7 THINGS A PARENT LOVES IN A TEENAGER

The Bible tells us that a wise child will make one's father happy, but a foolish child will cause one's mother grief. (Prov. 10:1.) The attitudes and actions you display in your home have a major influence on the happiness of your family.

Here are 7 things you can do to bring joy in your family.

1. Do your chores without someone asking you to do them.

2. Offer to help with something around the house that is not usually your responsibility.

3. Think of a compliment you can give your mom, dad, or both.

4. Ask your parents if there is anything you can do to improve your behavior.

5. When asked to do something, don't procrastinate even a minute—go right to it.

6. If you have a brother or sister, treat your sibling with the same respect that you would want in return.

7. Be polite, thoughtful, and helpful outside of your home, at school, and in other activities.

6 KEYS TO BEING PROMOTED BY YOUR BOSS

No one likes to work at a job without being recognized and even promoted for one's labor. There are reasons why some people seem to climb the ladder of promotion and authority, while others remain on the lowest rung.

Here are 6 keys to your promotion at your work.

1. Always arrive a few minutes early for work and then stay at least a few minutes late.

2. Do not allow personal issues or other relationships at your job to take time or focus away from your work.

3. Never complain about your pay. You agreed to work for that amount, so be grateful!

4. Ask your boss from time to time if there is anything you can do to improve your performance.

5. Work with your head, not just your hands. Think of ways to do your job more effectively.

6. Don't continually badger your boss with requests for promotions or raises. Let your work do the talking,

pray, and trust God; and when the timing is right, ask to speak to your boss, without being demanding.

5 REGRETS NO TEEN SHOULD EVER LIVE WITH

The world is full of people who look back with regret on their teenage years. They longingly wish they had done things differently. You have the opportunity right now to assure yourself of no regrets.

Here are 5 regrets you don't want to live with the rest of your life.

1. **Moral regrets.** Don't allow yourself to compromise your purity and be remembered forever with the stains of sexual sin. (Rom. 12:1.)

2. **Ministry regrets.** If the Lord is speaking to you about sharing your faith with a classmate, take the opportunity. It may never come again.

3. **Mentor regrets.** Submit yourself to a good pastor and others you trust to mold you and develop you as a leader. Now is your greatest time of learning and personal development.

4. **Maximum regrets.** Never leave yourself wondering what could have happened—in school, athletics,

church, or any other part of life—if you would have given all you had to give to succeed.

5. **Media regrets.** Don't ever allow yourself to look back at your youth as a time when all you did was watch TV, play video games, and go to movies. Do something productive in your life, along with your entertainment.

7 QUESTIONS TO ASK YOUR PARENTS
IN THE NEXT 7 DAYS

Asking questions is a great way to learn and grow. You gain a perspective on areas of your life that you may have never realized. Here are 7 questions to ask your parents in the next 7 days. Look closely and learn as you read each answer.

1. How can I be a better son or daughter?

2. What do you see as my greatest strengths?

3. What do you think are the weaknesses that I must work on?

4. What friends do you see as the best influences in my life?

5. What kind of career could you see me getting into after I graduate?

6. When do I make you most proud?

7. What is the most important thing you've learned in life?

6 THINGS TO KNOW BEFORE YOU
BREAK THE LAW

The Bible says in Romans 13:1-2 that every person should be subject to a governing authority and that our resisting that authority will bring judgment on us. Here are 6 things you should know if you break the law, whether it is exceeding a speed limit or taking something that belongs to someone else.

1. God is bound by His Word to back up those who establish the laws, not you.

2. Even if you are not caught immediately, the consequences will eventually catch up with you.

3. Know what living on the inside of a 4' x 6' prison cell feels like, because that will be your future home.

4. Go down to the local jail and meet the criminals. If you choose to break the law, they could be your best friends.

5. Get a job making 50 cents an hour. That's about what they'll pay you in prison.

6. Realize that smaller violations will slowly but surely lead you to larger ones. It will become a downward spiral that is difficult to recover from.

[SUCCESS]

8 GOALS TO REACH BEFORE YOU'RE 18

At every stage in life, it is important to learn to set incremental goals towards the fulfillment of your dreams and vision. I encourage you to write your goals down as a regular reference point for your progress. Here are 8 goals to consider attaining before you're 18.

1. Make a long-term financial investment in the stock market.

2. Read the Bible through entirely.

3. Hold down one job for at least 6 months—a year if possible.

4. Read Dale Carnegie's book *How to Win Friends and Influence People.*

5. Obtain a basic idea of what career direction you are going to take, and make the necessary plans for school or training.

6. Develop one strong friendship that you will keep for life, no matter where you both end up.

7. Save enough money to buy a decent used car.

8. Keep your grades up, and get your high school diploma.

4 SUREFIRE WAYS TO
DISCOVER YOUR TALENTS

Proverbs 18:16 NKJV says, "A man's gift makes room for him, and brings him before great men." The discovery and implementation of your gifts and talents will bring you the success your heart desires.

Here are 4 ways to uncover your talents.

1. Ask those you know and trust what they see as your greatest talents.

2. Pray and ask God to reveal your gifts and talents to you. Jeremiah 33:3 promises that if we call on God, He'll show us hidden things which we don't know about.

3. Follow your heart's desires, and try new things. The results may surprise you.

4. Be faithful in little things you're asked to do, even if they aren't on your list of favorites. God tells us that if we're faithful in small things, we will be rulers over much. (Matt. 25:23.)

7 PERSONAL BELIEFS THAT
WILL ALTER YOUR FUTURE

Without a doubt, the most important thing you can establish in your life right now is what you believe. Your core convictions will separate you from the pack.

Here are 7 beliefs from the Bible that, if acted on, will alter your future for good.

1. I believe I am God's child and He is my Father. (1 John 3:1.)

2. I believe the Holy Spirit leads me in all my decisions. (Rom. 8:14.)

3. I believe I am more than a conqueror in every challenge life brings. (Rom. 8:37.)

4. I believe God is the author of my promotion in every area of life. (Ps. 75:6,7.)

5. I believe that when I pray, God hears me and answers me. (Mark 11:24.)

6. I believe that as I meditate on God's Word, He makes my way prosperous. (Josh. 1:8.)

7. I believe that nothing is impossible because I believe.
   (Mark 9:23.)

5 GOOD HABITS THAT WILL
MAKE YOU A WINNER

1. **Preparation.** "I will do all I must before, so that I can enjoy the results after."

2. **Action.** "I will do what I need to do right now because tomorrow may be too late."

3. **Prayer.** "I realize that my destiny is too great for me to attempt alone. God will be my constant help and source of strength to fulfill my dreams and achieve my destiny."

4. **Character.** "I will live life with honesty and integrity, the kind of attributes that will not just get me to the top, but keep me there."

5. **Discipline.** "I will continue to do what it takes to succeed, even when the excitement has dwindled, the new has worn off, and things become routine."

5 BAD HABITS THAT WILL LABEL YOU A LOSER

Whether in sports, school, or a career, there are decisions that will form habits and cause any person to come out on the losing end most of the time. Success and failure are not mysteries. You can choose either one.

Here are 5 habits to choose to refuse in your life.

1. **Finger pointing.** "It's someone else's fault that I didn't do well—not my own."

2. **Procrastination.** "I'll get to it later when the mood hits me just right and the universe comes into proper alignment."

3. **Unbelief.** "I don't think I was meant to succeed—mediocrity is just in my genes."

4. **Jealousy.** "I don't see why they get everything going their way. They get all the breaks."

5. **Laziness.** "I'm going to do the very least I have to do in order to get this job done. So what if it's not my best?"

ENDNOTES

[1] Strong, James, *The New Strong's Exhaustive Concordance of the Bible,* "Greek." Nashville: Thomas Nelson Publishers, 1990, s.v. "communion," entry #2842.

MEET BLAINE BARTEL

Past: Came to Christ at age 16 on the heels of the Jesus movement. While in pursuit of a professional freestyle skiing career, answered God's call to reach young people. Developed and hosted groundbreaking television series *Fire by Nite*. Planted and pastored a growing church in Colorado Springs.

Present: Serves under his pastor and mentor of nearly 20 years, Willie George, senior pastor of 12,000-member Church on the Move in Tulsa, Oklahoma. Youth pastor of Oneighty®, America's largest local church youth ministry, and reaches more than 1,500 students weekly. National director of Oneighty's® worldwide outreaches, including a network of over 400 affiliated youth ministries. Host of Elevate, one of the largest annual youth leadership training conferences in the nation. Host of *Thrive*™, youth leader audio resource series listened to by thousands each month.

Passion: Summed up in 3 simple words: "Serving America's Future." Life quest is "to relevantly introduce the person of Jesus Christ to each new generation of young people, leaving footprints for future leaders to follow."

Personal: Still madly in love with his wife and partner of 20 years, Cathy. Raising 3 boys who love God, Jeremy—17, Dillon—15, and Brock—13. Avid hockey player and fan, with a rather impressive Gretzky memorabilia collection.

To contact Blaine Bartel,

write:

Blaine Bartel
Serving America's Future
P.O. Box 691923
Tulsa, OK 74169
www.blainebartel.com

*Please include your prayer requests
and comments when you write.*

To contact Oneighty®, write:

Oneighty®

P.O. Box 770

Tulsa, OK 74101

www.Oneighty.com

OTHER BOOKS BY BLAINE BARTEL

Ten Rules to Youth Ministry and Why Oneighty®
Breaks Them All

every teenager's
Little Black Book
on sex and dating

every teenager's
Little Black Book
on cool

every teenager's
Little Black Book
on cash

PRAYER OF SALVATION

A born-again, committed relationship with God is the key to a victorious life. Jesus, the Son of God, laid down His life and rose again so that we could spend eternity with Him in heaven and experience His absolute best on earth. The Bible says, "For God so loved the world, that he gave his only begotten Son, that whosoever believeth in him should not perish, but have everlasting life" (John 3:16).

It is the will of God that everyone receive eternal salvation. The way to receive this salvation is to call upon the name of Jesus and confess Him as your Lord. The Bible says, "That if thou shalt confess with thy mouth the Lord Jesus, and shalt believe in thine heart that God hath raised him from the dead, thou shalt be saved. For whosoever shall call upon the name of the Lord shall be saved" (Romans 10:9,13).

Jesus has given salvation, healing, and countless benefits to all who call upon His name. These benefits can be yours if you receive Him into your heart by praying this prayer:

Heavenly Father, I come to You admitting that I am a sinner. Right now, I choose to turn away from sin, and I ask You to cleanse me of all unrighteousness. I believe that Your Son, Jesus, died on the cross to take away my sins. I also believe that He rose again from the dead so that I may be justified and made righteous through faith in Him. I call upon the name of Jesus Christ to be the Savior and Lord of my life. Jesus, I choose to follow You, and I ask that You fill me with the power of the Holy Spirit. I declare right now that I am a born-again child of God. I am free from sin, and full of the righteousness of God. I am saved in Jesus' name, amen.

If you have prayed this prayer to receive Jesus Christ as your Savior, or if this book has changed your life, we would like to hear from you. Please write us at:

Harrison House Publishers

P.O. Box 35035

Tulsa, Oklahoma 74153

You can also visit us on the Web at

www.harrisonhouse.com

Additional copies of this book
are available from your local bookstore.

HARRISON HOUSE

Tulsa, Oklahoma 74153

THE HARRISON HOUSE VISION

Proclaiming the truth and the power
Of the Gospel of Jesus Christ
With excellence;

Challenging Christians to
Live victoriously,
Grow spiritually,
Know God intimately.